To Planet Earth, its inhabitants and future generations.

This edition published by Silver Quill Publishing 2020
First published by Royal Publishing House 2017

ISBN: 978-1-912513-74-1   Order Number: 194634

Text copyright © Sheikha Shamma bint Sultan bin Khalifa Al Nahyan – 2017
Illustrations copyright © Dr. Dianne Breeze – 2017
Typography and layout copyright © Ellen Covey – 2017
Photograph of Maxima taken by N.Katz

Sheikha Shamma bint Sultan bin Khalifa Al Nahyan asserts the
moral right to be identified as the author of this work

All rights reserved. No part of this publication may be reproduced, stored in or introduced into a retrieval system, or transmitted, in any form, or by any means (electronic, mechanical, photocopying, recording or otherwise), without the prior written permission of the publisher. Any person who does any unauthorised act in relation to this publication may be liable to primal prosecution and civil claims for damages.

The Adventures of Maxima and Coustaud
In Search of a Global Solution

"'In Search of A Global Solution' introduces children to the dangers of climate change and, most importantly, what they can do to stop it, observing their environment and listening to others."

Kathy Calvin
Chief Executive Officer, United Nations Foundation

"A gift for the future – stories that help children to love and care for our precious planet."

Dame Polly Courtice
Director, Cambridge Institute of Sustainability Leadership

"This wonderful story teaches children about the consequences of their actions, and the importance of protecting their planet. Maxima and Coustaud's magical journey will inspire young readers all around the world to be more conscious global citizens."

His Excellency Dr Thani Al Zeyoudi
Minister of Climate Change and Environment, UAE

"This delightful book, with its great characters and exciting adventures, encourages young readers to think about the environmental impact of human activities, and helps them to consider how they can support a more sustainable future for our planet. We hope that Maxima and Coustaud continue their wonderful journey of respect for Mother Nature."

Mohamed Jameel Al Ramahi
Chief Executive Officer, Masdar

Once upon a time in a land not so far away,
there was a tall, old tree that stood out
in the middle of a magnificent forest.

It was covered with luminous green
leaves and fiery red blossoms that
could be seen from **space**.

Mother Tree of Hope, as she was
called, was not an ordinary tree; not
only was she home to many creatures
but she had a wise, deep voice and two
unusual ears that listened to everyone.

She, like **all the trees** on Planet Earth, gives life to all of us ...

... for trees give us **the oxygen we breathe!**

Coustaud, a small and strange-looking black dog, was walking through the forest with his best friend, a horse called **Magical Maxima**, at his side.

Coustaud looked up at Maxima.

"Why don't we go and see our friend, Mother Tree of Hope?"

"Yes, it's been a while since we last visited her," replied Maxima.

"Tally ho, let's go!"

She lay on the ground so that Coustaud could jump onto her back…

one, two, three, hop!

Coustaud smiled proudly.

"YAY! It's getting easier and easier to climb on your back."

"The **more** you practise, the **easier** it gets!" replied Maxima.

When they reached Mother Tree, they saw a white creature with big spiral curls lying beside her.

Maxima greeted the strange animal. "Hello there!"

The creature replied in a s l o w, sad voice.

"Bo... Bo..."

Maxima rolled her eyes and looked at it closely.
Filled with curiosity, she asked,
"What are you doing here?
What's your name?"

She realised that the creature was a sheep,
but all it could say was "Bo…Bo…"
An **unusual** sound for a sheep!

Coustaud scratched his head,
wondering what had made
the sheep's voice disappear.

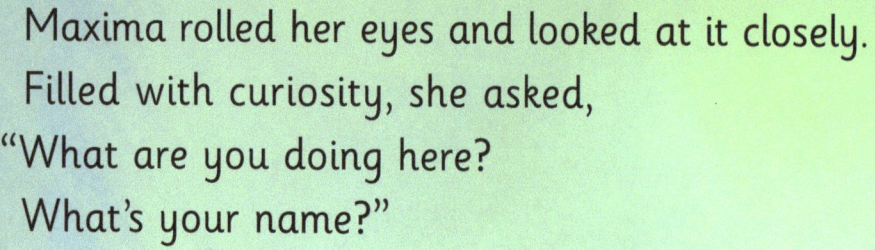

Mother Tree of Hope began to speak in her wise, deep voice. "Hello Maxima and Coustaud, I haven't seen you two for a very long time."

Then she explained that the sad sheep was called Bobo and had been sitting there for the last three days feeling very miserable. He was unable to communicate because he had lost his voice.

Maxima was very worried. "What exactly has happened to Bobo's voice?" she asked, fearing the worst.

Mother Tree hesitated for a moment before replying.
"I think it must be something to do with The Wicked Witch."

At these words, Coustaud jumped back
in fright and fell **splat** into a muddy puddle.

Maxima and Mother Tree watched
the little dog stand up again with

gruesome, gooey, glumpy mud

dripping off him.

Poor Coustaud was very **smelly** now
and looked like a pile of horse poo.

Maxima was very concerned as Mother Tree explained that they needed to find Bobo's voice box before it was too late.

"**Too late?**" said the horrified horse. "**Why?**"

"The world is getting hotter and if we don't do something now, then we will lose Bobo's voice box forever and we will all suffer the consequences. We'll no longer hear the voices of all the sheep in the world and we won't be able to protect our planet."

Maxima was puzzled.
"What do you mean?"

"Some humans are over-farming, and so animals such as sheep are unknowingly causing Planet Earth to **heat up**," she explained.

Maxima looked up at her.
"What advice can you give us, Mother Tree?"

"I would start by looking on the outskirts of the enchanted forest. I think humans have been cutting down trees there. I can hear their machinery getting **louder** and **louder**, which means they're getting closer and closer. With no trees, the place we all inhabit will be too hot to live in."

Maxima was raring to go and took off at once, **flying high over the forest.**

Coustaud held on to her mane for dear life and her long hair blew back into his mouth. He spat it out. "Eeuuw! What shampoo did you wash your hair with, Maxima?"

The duo stopped amongst the trees
to ask the lumberjacks if they had seen
a voice box. The workers answered, "**No!**"

They left disappointed, but this time they flew over
the deep, blue sea and spoke to the turtles.

"Have you seen a voice box?" asked Coustaud.

"**NO**" replied the turtles.

As they were about to leave, one of the turtles stopped them.

"Please can you help me before you go? Can you take me out of this plastic bag? Humans have been throwing their garbage into the sea and we need help. This bag is weighing me down and I can no longer swim."

Maxima and Coustaud quickly removed the bag and the turtle did a happy little dance, flapping his flippers.

"Thank you," he said. "Don't stop helping anyone in need – the **whole** planet and animal kingdom need you."

They took off again, soaring into the sky, heading for the Arctic Circle.

As they drew near, Coustaud's coat began to grow **thicker** and his jaws trembled uncontrollably.

"BRrRRr," he said. "It's **freezing** over here!"

"Hello, Pinga the polar bear! Have you seen a voice box?" asked Maxima hopefully.

The polar bear replied in a disappointed tone. "It was on the ice, but when the ice caps **melted** I saw it float away into the distance."

So, off they went and this time they decided they should discuss the problem with **all** living beings – humans, plants and animals.

"Do you think it will work?" asked Coustaud. "You always need to have **hope** that a solution can be found," said Maxima.

So everyone sat on a bright star overlooking Planet Earth, trying to come up with a solution.

"Deforestation is making Planet Earth **unbearably hot**," said the trees.

"Humans need to do something about it."

"The Earth is getting hotter," said the polar bears.

"The ice where we live is melting and without ice there will be no more polar bears."

"Humans need to do something about it."

"Litter is causing us and our friends in the sea to get hurt," said the turtles.

"Humans need to do something about it."

The humans listened carefully to all the other living beings.

"**We will change** to make sure that we can all live together in harmony," they said.

After the meeting, things started to get **better**.

The polar bear cubs had a **wonderful** time playing in the snow, the turtles enjoyed swimming again, the trees were happy, and the birds decided to help by bringing back Bobo's **voice box**.

Filled with relief that the outcome of the meeting was so positive, Maxima gave Coustaud an **enormous** *hug.*

"Can you believe it wasn't the Wicked Witch, but instead it was humans who were responsible for Bobo losing his voice box?" said Coustaud. "I think I **scared** her so much last time we met her that she wouldn't **dare** do anything else."

Maxima rolled her eyes and giggled as she remembered their previous adventure when they saved the lost princess.

A happier, perkier sheep once again, Bobo twirled round and round in circles, singing **beautifully**. His voice and the voice of his people could now be heard.

Coustaud broke into a dance and started **showing off** as he told the tale of his leadership ability to bring people together.

Everyone on Planet Earth lived happily ever after, in peace and harmony with one another.

"Be kind to the Planet you live on, young readers!" says Coustaud.

In loving memory of Coustaud who will live on
in the hearts and minds of children who accompany him
and Maxima on their adventures.

Maxima

of

Coustaud

www.ingramcontent.com/pod-product-compliance
Lightning Source LLC
Chambersburg PA
CBHW041500220426
43661CB00016B/1202